DISCOVERING DESTINY

A 31-Day Guide to Discovering Yourself and Fulfilling Your Purpose

DESTINY | INSPIRE

Destiny Inspire

Discovering Destiny

31 – Day Guide to Finding Yourself and Fulfilling Your Purpose

Published by Destiny Inspire LLC

Augusta, Ga

www.destinyinspire.com

ISBN 978-1-62676-732-4

CONTENTS

Introduction V

Dedication VII

Day 1 Identity 1

Day 2 Uncover To Discover 5

Day 3 Clarity And Transparency 8

Day 4 Reveal And Heal... 12

Day 5 Launch Or Leap 15

Day 6 Passion And Purpose.. 19

Day 7 Perspective Thoughts 22

Day 8 Empowering The Purpose 26

Day 9 Preserving Your Peace....................................... 29

Day 10 Parting With The Plan...................................... 33

Day 11 Fixed Focus 37

Day 12 From Comparison To Completion 41

Day 13 Mission Matters 45

Day 14 Alignment With The Assignment...................... 48

Day 15 Purposed Over Popular 51

Day 16 Conquering Comfort 54

Day 17 Disposing Of Distractions 57

Day 18 Selfless To Selfish 61

Day 19 More Than Mediocre 66

Day 20 Grind And Grow 70

Day 21 Strength From The Struggle 74

Day 22 Push Past It 78

Day 23 The Patience Process....................................... 81

Day 24 Dear Dreamer 85

Day 25 Higher Heights... 89

Day 26 Turning Points... 92

Day 27 Correct Connections 95

Day 28 Live The Legacy.. 99

Day 29 Private Party..103

Day 30 Destination Discovery...107

Day 31 The Reciprocation...110

Special Acknowledgements To A Few Very Special People.......113

INTRODUCTION

D o you find yourself swaying between who you are and who you should be? Do you struggle with the necessary steps to achieve your life purpose? There was a time when I reluctantly found myself answering yes to these very questions. I was torn between who I thought I should be and who society and my environment had influenced me to be. It wasn't until I finally made the decision to take control of my life and live out my destiny on my own terms, that I began to experience the fulfillment and joy I had been missing my whole life. I was no longer stuck in the dilemma of discovering who I was.

In *A 31-Day Guide to Discovering Yourself and Fulfilling Your Purpose*, I share how discovering your destiny starts with first discovering your identity. I also share the principles that have helped me grow not only into the woman I am today, but also into my divine purpose.

By the time you finish reading this book, you will be able to clarify what's preventing you from living a life based on purpose. You will also be empowered to create the life you both desire and deserve as you learn how to build the character that will sustain you wherever your destiny takes you.

DEDICATION

Special thanks to my parents for your love, prayers, and steadfastness. You have unselfishly and patiently been by my side during this journey of self-discovery.

To my father who is indeed the greatest man I've ever known. Very few men demonstrate the integrity and faith I've seen in you. I'm the woman I am today because of your wisdom and abundant love. Your unconditional love and understanding of my journey were some of the driving forces that afforded me the liberty to find myself and fulfill my purpose.

To my mom who has been patient and loving in all my circumstances. Thank you for showing me how to be a woman of grace, grind, and grit. I have watched you go after everything you said you would accomplish.

To the one person who pushed me, and inspired me to create this legacy and to keep fighting until the finish, thank you!

Lastly, I dedicate this book to every person who has longed for the day of waking up and pursuing the plan God has for your life. This is to every queen who has fought to hold on, no matter how hard life tried to pull her away. Also, to every king who didn't let his journey kill his joy! May your inner strength and beauty of your spirit continue to radiate brighter than the sun. May this book allow you to continue persevering until your purpose is revealed and fulfilled

DAY 1

IDENTITY

I want to start this day off by asking the very question that led to the creation of this guide. Who exactly are you? Take a moment and think deeply about this question. Write it out as a list if you must. Then take another moment and allow the answer to fully resonate. When I ask who you are, I'm not referring to your name or the identity you are by. Most people answer this question by looking from the outside in. I don't want you to answer the question from the perspective of an onlooker, but from the inside looking out.

I must be very transparent and let you know that there was a season in my life when I struggled with finding the answer to this question. The irony about it is that there was once a time when I thought I had the answer solidified. When the pieces of the identity I created started to break away, I began to see myself self-destruct. It wasn't until I made the decision to live in my truth that I began dismantling what I misguidedly thought was my established truth. This was also when I went back to the starting point of my life. I began to cleanse myself of who I allowed my environment and others to convince me that I was; and I set out to find the answer to my very own question once and for all.

What about you?

If you are someone who also defines yourself based on outside factors, then it's with most profound regret that I inform you that you're sadly mistaken. Think back for a moment on the list you made to define your identity. Now ponder on this just for a moment. What if everything you named was all stripped away in the blink of an eye? What then would be left to make up who you say you are?

We identify our self-worth by our titles, roles, responsibilities and sometimes even by our possessions. I labeled myself as just a wife, worker, secretary, etc. Once the conditions of those titles changed, so did I. I was so consumed with maintaining the titles in order to maintain my identity that I never realized I had already lost myself.

Never allow what you do and what you have to take precedence over who you truly are.

Yes, you may be a parent by choice, a spouse by marriage, a business person by profession; and you may consider yourself to be wealthy, popular, or even poor, but none of this can embody the true essence of the real you on the inside. You are so much more than these things. You are a person with a purpose greater than anything man could create or make up.

Who are you not?

Before I could pinpoint who I was, I had to start ruling out who I was not. I knew I was not the sum of my problems, circumstances, and past failures. I also knew I was not worthless. Although I sometimes experienced rough depression, I was not going to accept depression as part of who I was. I knew that wasn't who I was meant to be. Many times I felt like I was at my wits end, yet I had to tell myself, "Girl, you are not crazy." I went ahead and knocked out all the other negative things I allowed others to convince me of. I was not any of that.

So maybe you need to start with the process of elimination and rule out everything and everyone you are not. Doing this will help you to create a new list to remind yourself of who you are. You were made perfect and with a purpose. Don't let life steal that identity away from you.

Ask yourself:

1. Who was I before life, problems, and people changed that?

3

2. Apart from my roles, titles, or responsibilities, what else do I define myself as?

3. List the characteristics and attributes you feel make up the real you.

4. Who is it that you are striving to be?

5. What do you hope to accomplish as a result of reading this guide?

DAY 2

UNCOVER TO DISCOVER

As a child my brother and I would hide things in our parents' backyard just for fun. We would later try to find the "x" marking the spot and begin digging it up again. Just as it was when I was child, there is still something exhilarating about discovering something unique, unexpected, or even forgotten. What I've come to realize is that anything deemed to be of great value is either kept in a secure place or hidden. It is never just lying on the surface in plain sight. It's usually discovered in a crack, crevice, or hiding spot waiting to be unearthed; and remains hidden until a worthy recipient comes along to put in the work required to dig it out.

I compare the discovery of finding the "x" to our destiny. This is a treasure far more priceless; and before our fate and gifts can be discovered, they must first be unleashed from what keeps them hidden.

The Issue

Oftentimes we desperately want to unveil our gift, talent, and contribution to the world. This is such a beautiful thing, but the problem lies in the fact that we haven't removed the dirt and debris covering them up. The "x" we are trying to get to is buried deep beneath all the issues, insecurities, and concerns we have not dealt with. You must penetrate through everything that has been lying dormant on the surface of your life. It's time to take the shovel of self-evaluation and dig up some of the things you thought could stay hidden. This is all part of learning who you are and what allows you function correctly.

When you don't correctly handle the underlining issues within, these things begin to unconsciously surface when you least expect them to. Just when you think life is finally at a place of stability or normalcy, the very things you did not root up will spring up to destroy what you have grown.

Possibilities

By now I hope you've asked yourself, "What could that one thing be that's hindering me?" It is the very thing you've been suppressing, avoiding, and ignoring. Sometimes it is the dirt of rejection, failure, loss, fear, pain, doubt, pity, abuse, insecurity, stubbornness, or just a bad attitude. The list can go on. So I want you to write yours out. It's time to confess it, so you can begin to correct it.

Today is all about dismantling the dirt of your heart and sifting through the soil of your soul. This journey is going to require you to cultivate confidence and also build character. Having strong character will be a reoccurring element, and will help you in discovering the life you desire and truly deserve. As I recently told a class of business students, "Don't let career take you where your character can't keep you." Take the time to uncover what's stopping your growth, so that you can start getting clear on what's next.

Ask yourself:

1. What secret struggles are you dealing with that you need to address?

2. How has this hindered your growth?

DAY 3

CLARITY AND TRANSPARENCY

If you've ever played the game of Poker or been around the game, you know that the sign of a great player is their ability to maintain a stoic disposition regardless of their predicament. Whether their hand is exceptionally favorable or not, they want the table to be unclear as to what is going on in their head and ignorant to what's in their hand. This is done in hopes of maintaining the "upper hand" at all times. The objective is not to allow others to see through you by your emotions. Now, in a game of Texas Hold 'Em, this ideal way of thinking is handy. Consequently, when this same way of thinking is used in the game of life, the results don't always pan out with the same level of success and effectiveness.

We walk around wearing our inscrutable smiles painted on to perfection, when in reality we need help reaching our goals. We need help to overcome life's issues; and we need help in areas we are unaware requires help. We are unclear in so many areas of our life, yet we make it appear otherwise. We want to look as if we have it all together and don't need assistance from anyone. I've been very guilty of this myself.

Here's a Tip: Never use a poker face to create a façade for things you don't want to face.

The problem with creating these opaque personas is that it doesn't allow us to be honest with ourselves. Once you have gained clarity on who you are, clarify what it is that you want and then formulate a plan of action to accomplish it.

How did I do it?

I had to become clear on where I was currently in life, accept it, and if I didn't like it, work towards changing it.

This started with finding the freedom in just being me. I was one of those people who took my issues and hid them behind my best, "Oh, I'm good." I feared that if my flaws became visible to others, they would be seen as failure. I needed so desperately to maintain the picture of perfection others had been accustomed to seeing. If I didn't, I could be pushed down from the same pedestal I had been put on—one that I never particularly desired to be on to begin with.

I eventually removed my poker face, and let my guard down just enough to position myself around those I knew would be an asset to my growth and progress. This meant finding mentors, coaches, and even searching for a type of therapy that did not consist of retail. Here's a secret I learned in this, It's ok to pray for peace, but actually pay someone to help you find it. You'll be surprised how much insight it can provide you.

It became clear to me that I needed others to be influenced by my flaws as well as my fortitude. Without the two of them put together, I ceased to be truly effective at being me. Becoming transparent allowed me to find the platform for my purpose, which is impacting those who are reading this guide right now. I realized that no one can be impacted by the version of who you're pretending to be.

The Bigger Picture

I know you may think the whole purpose of this guide revolves around you. The part about finding yourself does. However, the truth is, discovering your destiny is not all about you. There's a lot more to it. It's about learning how to live an abundant and fulfilled life that will in return enhance the lives of others around you. We are all put on this earth as the solution to some type of problem. You must be transparent enough to work on your problems first, but don't stop there. Until you can gain clarity and discover the problem that you are the answer to, it will always be difficult to pursue your goals.

Ask Yourself:

1. Do you fear being yourself or being accepted by others?

2. What areas of your life could you use more clarity in?

3. What is it that you want to achieve with your life?

4. Who is the go to person in your life?

DAY 4

REVEAL AND HEAL

If you have ever visited a doctor's office with severe pain or sickness, one of the first questions posed is either, "What's the problem?" or "Where is the pain?" The presence of either suggests that you alone have the key to what will happen next. The revealing of trouble or pain will allow the physician to accurately assess and test the necessary areas, thereby eliminating non-contributing factors.

The same is true before pursuing anything. You have to lay some groundwork and begin asking questions. Without exposing the root of a problem, it prolongs the process, thereby making the healing a lot more difficult. We discussed how to dig and uncover our dirt to get to our treasure. Now, we have to work on healing it.

I thought it would be much easier to suppress depression as if somehow it would miraculously disappear. As a way to overcompensate, I hid my weaknesses by exposing my strengths. One day I had to realize my wounds weren't going to heal until I admitted they were hurting.

When you conceal the issues holding you back instead of deciding to deal with them, you restrict yourself from moving forward and seeing the more precise picture. Finding the root of it all is the first step to healing.

Sometimes we believe the revelation of our flaws and failures will in some way set us up for rejection from others. True enough, there are those who cannot handle what you're hiding, but there are also those who are in your life to provide protection and provision for these very things. However, if your heart is not open, you won't be able to accept what's set up to help heal you.

This extends to healing from things that may have been done to you by others in the past. The offense may not have been your fault, but the responsibility to heal from it is all yours. You only victimize yourself when you walk around carrying things you have no control over, instead of controlling what you can control.

Sometimes we even operate in positions where we are the support system and comforter to others. You can't possibly bring successful and effective healing to others until you deal, reveal, and ultimately heal yourself.

As you see, the first few days have all been about working from the inside-out. We have to get that right first before we can get the rest. The challenge to you is to continue the self-assessment, which by now I'm certain you have already begun. With surety, search out the answer to the physician's original question, "Where is the pain?" Once you've found it and worked on it, then we can step out and move forward.

Ask Yourself:

1. Have I taken the time to do an inventory of issues or problems that haven't been addressed?

2. What triggers or signs may be an indication that healing needs to take place in my life?

3. What are necessary steps that I need to take to help facilitate my healing? Does this included seeking out therapy or mentorship?

DAY 5

LAUNCH OR LEAP

What's the one thing lying dormant in the crevice of your heart that you have yet to act on? Could it be applying for that job or promotion? Maybe it's that business that would allow you to change your passion for profiting. Is it time to venture into a new partnership or relationship? Is it obtaining that degree that you either never finished or never began? For some, it can be taking the time to build the new life and family of your dreams. Is that still not you? Maybe it's as simple as cutting the necessary ties to begin again. Whatever might be presented to you, ask yourself, is it time to finally launch out or leap out further?

Its Time!

The time has come for you to close that gap between where you are and where you need to be. We spend much of our time merely pondering the "what if's" in our life, instead of taking necessary action to dive into the daunting deep. Time spent wondering and waiting is equivalent to what it would have taken if you had decided to make a move. What exactly are you still waiting for? You are treating life as if you are on the playground, and you're double-dutching with your destiny! I'm yelling on the sidelines for you to *Jump In!*

It's time that you launched out! Don't worry about the details of how you will get it done in the end. Just formulate a plan to guide you. Everything about launching out is going to be a learning curve, so don't think you have to have everything perfect. I don't even want you to stress yourself if you fail because with perseverance you WILL eventually fly. You need to make the decision.

What if I told you that everything you have ever imagined is on the other side of everything you don't want to do?

Let's say you have successfully launched out. You have gotten the courage to take that first step. Now you have to keep going as far as your journey will lead. Don't settle for where you are when you know there is more. All you need to do is leap! Is it risky? Yes, it is! Intimidating? Absolutely! So, would you rather stay stagnant or steadily moving? Don't stop because you've gotten a little progress, because I'm sure there is more for you to do.

Walking on Water

I always say, "If I'd never stepped out of the boat, I would never have known I could walk on water." Was the water cold? Yes, very cold and even shallow. However, it was my intuition and courage yelling at me to *DO IT ANYWAY!* Everything I'm doing now is a result of decisions I made way back. These decisions came from being tired of always wondering what life could or would be like if I took a chance on myself for a change. I made that one step of faith to launch out on a journey and started a blog, which later led me to leap a little further and write a book. Now, I get to travel all over inspiring and empowering others. It all started with making that one decision, despite my fear.

Leap

No, I didn't know all the coordinates, and I wasn't even sure of where I would land. But what I did have was the will to walk into something didn't, and to experience a new level. I'm still leaping to get to the other side of my destiny; and I'm doing it with confidence knowing that there's so much farther I have to go! I'm trying to help you bridge that gap from where you are, and where you want to be. For you that may be a simple as leaping to the other side, allowing your faith to be your wings.

The challenge is all yours. Will you stay on the shore? I'm praying as the days go on that this guide will inspire you to keep reaching and wanting more for your life. The only thing stopping you is you! Just make the decision.

Ask Yourself

1. What is the one thing you would do if you knew you could not fail?

2. What do you need to step out and do?

3. What is stopping you?

DAY 6

PASSION AND PURPOSE

What gives you an indescribable feeling when you think about it? What is it that makes that light bulb in your head go off? What drives you every morning that you wake up? What problem areas do you recognize in life that give you an insatiable desire to do something? Answering these questions will help with leading you in the right direction of your purpose.

New Oxford American Dictionary defines passion as a strong and barely controllable emotion. This is an emotion we tend to neglect and ignore without knowing that it can be the starting point of purpose. For me, my passion for expressing myself with words coupled with a sincere desire to help people led me to where I am now. Had I continued to suppress and control that passion, it would have continued to work against me living in purpose. Focus your passion in the most effective area of life and decide how you can utilize it.

Once you give in to your passion, you must perform everything you do with it. This is how you grow in that area. When you have consistently invested your whole self into something, and I mean entirely immersed yourself in it, you can't help but experience the growth and success that comes along with it.

Leave the Light on!

Now, don't feel discouraged when your passion for what you are doing seems to become a burden to others. Passion is like a light. The light will expose the dull places of those who have not fully committed themselves to function at a high level of passion. There will be many to tell you "You're doing too much." Or "That doesn't make sense." I need you to leave your light on and let it continue to lead you. Sometimes these are the same people whose light burned out while trying to reach their goals.

How so?

Whenever you have an end goal (purpose), it propels you to keep going. This is the reason so many people start with a burning flame for something in life that slowly digresses to a flicker. They exhaust their efforts with the passion but fall back because there was no purpose behind it. There is no real driving force. There must be something pushing you from behind. That something has to contain more than superficial reasons. To be effective, you must have a balance of both. Passion with no purpose has no point! Start by answering the questions mentioned in previous sections.

If you are uncertain about how to answer those questions, survey some close friends and family. Get their take on what they feel makes you passionate. You may notice a pattern or trend in their answers, and this may uncover something different for you.

Ask Yourself:

1. Have I answered the questions given at the beginning of this chapter? If not, these are the questions you should be asking yourself.

DAY 7

PERSPECTIVE THOUGHTS

D o you ever wake up in the morning feeling annoyed at the intimidating sound of the alarm clock, taunting you with what the day may bring? What is the first thought that comes to your mind? "Shoot! It's Monday again?" Usually, it's that first thought that will guide the trajectory of your entire day.

The energy and thoughts you put into the atmosphere will manifest into whatever you desire them to be. We are first spirit beings, and so we have the power to command things into existence from a single thought. When you begin the day by thinking about the heavy weight of all the things you must get done, your perspective of your day will undoubtedly be a negative one; and this will only cause your day to progressively grow worse. Practice using cognitive dissonance to replace that negative thought with a positive one. Affirmations are perfect for changing your perspective. Try telling yourself, "I'm going to have such a productive day getting things done." Immediately, you have set the course of your day to accomplish the same tasks, but with a positive perspective, thereby, generating the energy needed to carry you through the day. By doing this, what may seem to be a problem will turn into progress.

Don't Give In

We easily succumb to the first drop of negativity that comes our way. In doing this we create a breeding ground of negative reciprocity. The very intent of our thoughts transcends time and space to produce the desired outcome, whether it is a good or bad thought.

Sometimes we can even allow the perspective of others to become projected into our psyche. It is far too easy to let the doubts of others distract us from the destiny we are trying to discover. The perspective you should have should be based on the vision inside of you—a vision currently seen with your eyes alone. The expectation level of others to positively see what you have seen, but not yet manifested, is naturally going to be low. This should only increase your faith in the future, and not diminish it.

Things to remember:

1. Stop surrounding yourself with people who are in need of a serious perspective shift.

2. Only think about what you want manifested.

3. Don't practice self-sabotage by seeing things in your life in a negative light.

4. Understand that your thoughts will heavily influence your perspective, which in return will control your actions.

Don't believe me? Examine your last few outcomes. Now, see if there is a correlation between the thoughts you were thinking and the steps you took, and ultimately the results you received within that time.

You must think about where you are going on this journey and what it will take you to get there. Change how you see things and the things you see will begin to change. Subjugate thoughts of doubt, dismay, inferiority, failure, and whatever else plagues your mind. Now that you are aware of how you can improve your life by just adjusting your perspective, how will you choose to see your life?

Ask yourself:

1. What thoughts are currently hindering my growth?

2. What outcomes in my life can I positively change as a result of changing my perspective?

DAY 8

EMPOWERING THE PURPOSE

In school, I always thrived in the areas of literature, reading, and writing. (Hopefully, you've been able to deduce that from reading this book so far.) These were areas of interest to me, so as I grew I became increasingly better at them.

In just the opposite, math was a queen's kryptonite! I cringed just walking through the doors of a math class. I saw numbers as swarm around me as if I had walked right into a hive of my demise. The worst part of it all is that I continued to empower the problem instead of finding a way to push past it. I chose to neglect the true essence of why I was in school to begin with. The whole purpose was that I needed education to carry me over into life in general. It wasn't to highlight the flaws and weaknesses I faced. So instead of grasping the problem and finding a way to solve it, I began making it even more significant.

It's true that where your focus goes, your energy flows as well. We walk into problems, and we surrender all of our power to them. We dwell and linger in a land of sorrows and shortcomings when we were designed to live limitlessly. We become completely consumed with feeding into the problem, never realizing it's still going to be there when we are done. The only difference is that the issue becomes a much more significant burden than it initially was.

We exhaust so much energy into everything that is not working out in our favor, until we entirely extract life out of what we do want to work, which is the true purpose. For some of us, we do this in relation to our careers, our homes, or even our finances. Either way, the concept works the same.

Stop Magnifying what doesn't matter

To magnify something is to make it bigger or larger than it appears to be.

The challenges are to:

- Stop making the problematic situations in your life seem more extensive than they have to be.

- Begin unplugging yourself from your problems right at the source of.

- Take that same amount of energy and passion and pump it into the solutions that will benefit you.

- Use your power to pursue your purpose and not to promote the problem. If you don't, the negativity you choose to empower will overwhelm you.

Ask Yourself:

1. What problems am I empowering?

2. What steps will I take to counteract this?

DAY 9

PRESERVING YOUR PEACE

One of my favorite memories was a trip I took to the Bahamas. While there, I spent each of my mornings in meditation and serenity on my hotel balcony overlooking the shallow shores of the ocean. I soon began to feel as if all that was wrong in life didn't matter, neither did it even compare to the peace I was experiencing. At that moment, there was a level of tranquility unlike any other. I refer to it as my peaceful place. It is a place I constantly revisit in my mind when I need to preserve my peace.

With so much already at hand daily, it's easy for your mind to get swept away into the tumultuous waves of life, thereby taking your peace right with it. I learned that it's hard trying to live in purpose and not have any peace, so it's important to possess peace within when everything on the outside appears chaotic.

Disruptions

I'm sure there are several opposers of peace in your life that you can name. You must learn to gain control of these disruptions, if you are going to be the master of your peace. Some of these disruptions include:

- Bills

- Overthinking

- Overanalyzing

- Responsibilities

- Health concerns

- Family issues

- The past

- Thoughts of the future

- People

This list could go on.

In my personal experience, I've discovered the one thing I deem to be of utmost value to me, and that is my peace of mind! I can't even comprehend that there was ever a time that I willingly allowed people and other forces to take control of my peace. What I've learned is the value of making better decisions with who and what I let into my life to protect my peace at all costs.

Not having peace will strip you of the ability to make sound decisions surrounding anything in your life. It's like trying to navigate through a burning, smoke filled room. When you are not operating with peace, you tend to see every situation as cloudy and overwhelming. Instead of seeing situations for what they are, you'll see them for how they appear to you, and act accordingly. Like anything else, there is always a price for peace.

Sacrifice

Sometimes the price of peace is sacrificing the company of those who keep you in a state of confusion or vexation. It also entails not allowing yourself to be drawn into things that are beyond your control, because this too will strip you of your peace. Accept the reality of the circumstances for what they are. Some days, everything that you thought should work out, won't possibly go how you envisioned! You must be ok with that. Gain the ability to free yourself of whatever comes to torment your psyche.

Things you can do:

- Become aware of the things jeopardizing your mental well-being and emotional stability.

- Change what you can change.

- Be patient with the things you can't change.

- Know your limitations.

- Set aside time to meditate and reflect.

- Find your "peaceful place".

- Give space and time for everything that must be accomplished.

In other words, continue to choose your peace over your problems. You must make the conscious decision today to make peace a priority, instead of an option.

Ask yourself:

1. What is the number one thing in your life that is disrupting your peace the most?

2. Based on the information shared, what are some steps you can take to begin preserving your peace?

DAY 10

PARTING WITH THE PLAN

Have you ever come up with the perfect sure-fire plan that you couldn't wait to execute? It may have been something as simple as planning for an exciting weekend, or as detailed as planning a long-term goal for the future. Every aspect was carefully laid out to the most minute detail. If it was a really in-depth plan, maybe you even broke it down using the S.M.A.R.T. method. You remember learning about that right?

The SMART plan

You made sure it was Specific. You set up a system to be able to Measure your progress through the process. You knew it was Achievable and attainable. If anyone could make it happen, it would definitely be you. That alone was what made it Realistic. You even had a timeline to calculate precisely how much Time you would need to get it done. You had every level covered. Then boom! For some reason or another, everything you had perfectly planned and organized fell through, and you were faced with parting from the original plan because of the challenges that occurred. This instantly discouraged you.

Usually when something doesn't work out in our favor, it's because there is something better in our future. Purpose has a way of detouring us from what we think we desire. It's not always because we had it wrong, it's just purpose working for us, and not against us. In retrospect, you should be glad that many of the ideas you originally mapped out, didn't lead you to the destination in the end.

What Plans?

Consider the plans that others had for your life. No matter how hard you tried, somehow you felt like you couldn't carry them out. Be mindful that some preset paths were never meant for you to follow anyway. Stop pressuring yourself. I once had to rethink about the plan I thought was right for me. The one everyone else expected me to follow.

Think about that relationship you planned to be in for the long haul? I've been there too. Because it didn't work out, you were able to discover that just because they were a "good time" didn't mean they were qualified to be a "lifetime". Even that career you thought you wanted ended up leading you to discover something else instead. Although it did not conform to your original plan, it all still worked out according to the right plan.

The blessing!

We've become spoiled by thinking the answers to our plans and our prayers should always be yes. Sometimes no is a blessing that comes as a disguise. Certain rejections we face are part of our protection, so we can't get so attached to what we think is a "Master Plan". Plans can and will always change. When they do, just know that's perfectly ok.

There's an adage that says, "Man plans, God laughs." People often get discouraged when their seemingly "good plan" turns out to not be God's plan- the infallible Master Plan. So remember this, if your plan A fails, there are still 25 more letters (plans), in the alphabet. You will get to where you are purposed to be one way or another. Get comfortable with change and learn to accept it. Don't become so attached to a specific way you think something should be done, that you aren't able to make adjustments when necessary.

Ask yourself:

1. What plans have recently been altered in your life?

2. What did you do to deal with the change?

3. Moving forward, what are some ways you will adjust to unexpected changes?

DAY 11

FIXED FOCUS

If you've ever watched a horse race, you have likely seen the masks placed over each animal's face. I used to wonder what purpose they served and assumed they were just a part of the horse's poorly executed fashion ensemble. Don't judge me. Little did I know that these less than fashionable masks were serving a purpose far greater than I could have imagined. These masks are known as blinders or blinkers. Their sole purpose is to deter the horse from distractions while racing. They block them from seeing what is on their sides or what's taking place behind them. This makes for a more powerful race as the horses are able to block out outside interference, and focus and concentrate on what's before them. Without them, the horses can become very panicky and nervous from the distractions around them, and in turn be disastrous to them and their rider.

This road to discovery you're on is like that of a race horse's journey. If you're not careful while traveling this road, and if you don't keep your eyes fixated on the prize, in an instant a disaster can disrupt your motives. The multitude of thoughts and ideas swimming through your head, the various temptations surrounding you and the never-ending opinions of others will make it difficult to stay focused on just one thing. It doesn't help if you're trying to shift your focus to watch what others are doing.

Another part of losing focus can be attributed to the desire to accomplish so much in such little time. We know we are made to accomplish great feats, so we feel the need to take on so much more than what we were originally designed to handle. It's not to say that you can't accomplish all the things you have on your to-do list. It simply explains how the zeal and passion you begin with slowly dissipates as you try to master it all at once.

Key point to remember: Before you can go up, there are things you must give up. This doesn't mean you must give them up in totality. It means pacing yourself and realizing when it is the right time to take on certain things. Right now, to keep your focus, you have to find that one thing to focus on. It's never a good idea to try to be a Jack of all trades, yet a master of none. Focus on whatever you are focusing on.

Maybe for you, it's the unexpectedness of life that can force your focus to shift. It is in these awkward moments that you must create your blinders to stay calm and to keep you from becoming frantic. It is far too easy to panic when something unexpected comes from behind or beside us and tries to knock us out of the race. It is in these very moments that maintaining our flow and focus is key.

Ways to Fix It

- If there are multiple things you wish to do or accomplish, organize them into a list.

- Prioritize what is most important to you or most necessary.

- Focus on building that one thing before moving on to something else.

- Commit your all to whatever you are working on or trying to develop.

- Pace yourself.

- Try not to think about how much you must do. Just do what you are doing now!

Ask yourself:

1. Have you prioritized things in your life? If not, when do you plan to start?

2. What is breaking your focus right now?

3. What can you do today to start regaining your
    focus?

DAY 12

FROM COMPARISON TO COMPLETION

The massive influence of technology in this generation is amazingly mesmerizing. You can instantly connect with millions of other people around the world without ever leaving the comfort of your home. You can see what your favorite stars and celebrities are wearing, you can see what your friends are doing, and you can watch the lives of the insanely rich, famous, and foolish.

With such revolutionary creations in which we revolve our lives around, it's hard not to become consumed with the lives of others.

Having access to all this innovation has created a culture of comparison. From the time we wake up in the morning until the time we stay up late at night, we tire our fingers from scrolling through the streets of social media timelines and surfing through the channels of vastly growing television shows.

We are adaptive creatures, so we begin to produce what we have consumed. This comparison has turned into a need to compete. We simulate our lives and where we think we should be by the appearances of what we see and deem to be a representation of success. It seems as if everyone around you has found some purpose or reached a fantastic milestone. Then, there is you! Still trying to figure out who you are and who you want to be. Just like a horse without blinders, you may find yourself looking at the person next to you, which may cause you to run your race in their lane, instead of yours.

The Cost

When you adjust the plan based on the need to keep up and deviate from the original way, it will cost you valuable time and attention that could have been used on your path of success and fulfillment.

Comparison leads to incompletion. This is going to cost you peace and confidence in who you were designed to be. While you're busy watching someone else, you must keep in mind the divine design for your life. Your path and God's plan won't be the same as someone else's. You have no idea the cost someone else had to pay to get to where they are and to maintain the lane they are currently in. Is that a price you are willing to pay?

Results of comparing/competing

Believe me when I say comparison kills.

- It kills your hope of reaching your own goals.

- It halts your confidence because you can never fill someone else's shoes.

- It ruins your determination because it sometimes discourages you from even trying.

- It kills your drive to do what you were created to do.

Next time you're being schooled by life, and you feel tempted to look over into someone else's life and compare it to yours, remember this, just like each class in school is given a different assignment, each person in life is given a duty as well. Therefore, the tests given to you will differ from the trials of those around you. Your life has been created to revolve around the destination for your life. So if you are comparing and competing with what you see around you, you are not completing the job that is before you and inside of you.

Ask yourself:

1. Who or what are you secretly in competition with?

2. Do you know everything that someone else has gone through to get where they are?

3. Are you willing to go through the things others have gone through to get what they have?

4. What are some things you can be grateful for that you possess or that you have accomplished?

DAY 13

MISSION MATTERS

E very corporation or organization creates a mission statement that communicates various facets of what they do and who they are. This statement usually sums up what they hold as their values, clarifies their purpose, and identifies their objective and most importantly who they are. They often post them everywhere within their establishment; and many of us are drawn to these companies based on what they stand for, believe in, or represent.

Have you ever considered what the mission statement for your life is? If not, today is the right day and right time to start. Having a mission gives you something to work toward and also guides you as you're getting there. Part of my mission statement is empowering, impacting, and inspiring others to live in purpose.

Regardless of who you are and what capacity you function in within life, a personal mission statement is beneficial in helping you define who you are and sticking to what you want. Whether you are the CEO of a company, a student, or a loving parent trying to be the best parent you can be, having a personal mission statement will help you understand exactly who you are, where you want to go, and what you represent. This is a great motivator in helping to identify your purpose and pursue it.

Set It Up

You want to be as realistic as possible when creating your mission statement. It can be simple and summed up in a few sentences.

- List out your core values and your beliefs/principles.

- Find out what is important to you.

- Explore what gives you life or brings you the most joy.

- List out the skills or abilities you have naturally and/or that you have acquired.

- Ask yourself what you are passionate about.

- Think about the people you admire or look up to. Consider their impact and how it connects to you.

- How do you or how can you utilize your gifts, talents or abilities? Who can it help?

Reflect on the answers and put them all together. Write it all down to make it real. Keep your mission statement in plain sight. This will help manifest your purpose and vision from your head to your hands. Slowly, you will begin to formulate a pattern and a plan.

This mission statement will guide your actions to keep them in line with what you say you want. You may not have all the answers just yet in formulating your mission statement, but dedicate adequate time in creating one. All successful people have mission statements or vision statements for their lives. You should now be one of them.

Ask yourself:

1. Have you gained a better understanding of a personal mission statement?

2. If so, when do you plan to implement one? If not, what are you going to do to clarify it?

3. When do you plan to execute your mission statement?

DAY 14

ALIGNMENT WITH THE ASSIGNMENT

Part of the responsibility of owning a car is maintaining it. The time came for me to take my baby (my car) for its routine check-up. For a newer car, I thought I just needed an oil change, but to my surprise, the mechanic told me it was time to get an alignment. I thought maybe he was doing what most guys do when a woman comes in to get her car serviced, giving me more than what I asked for in hopes of finagling me out of more money. He began to explain to me that although my tires were new, to maintain the quality of my car and to get the best use of it, they would need to be rotated and re-aligned every few years. If not, driving my car would become more expensive as well as dangerous... how life itself can be viewed in a similar way.

We have all this drive, ambition, and potential, but when our goals and values are not in alignment with our purpose, we end up straying and swerving all over the place. This could cause damage and harm to ourselves and others.

Signs You're Not Aligned:

We create avenues to go down in life, which have absolutely nothing to do with our goals. We are connected to people who don't share or reflect our core values. We make decisions that will negatively impact the fulfillment of our purpose; and we become confused when all these routes lead us to dead ends. We're also hurt when the people we have invited into our lives to "help" us turn out to be destructive and counterproductive to our lives and our development.

When we don't channel our actions and thoughts to coincide with the desired outcome for our life directly, then what was meant to help us can end up harming us. As a result, a personal mission statement is essential as it will keep you in line with what you say you want to do and what you say you believe in.

Consider the areas of your life you are experiencing the most trouble. Decide if in some ways your actions are not in complete alignment with the divine assignment for your life. Being misaligned does not only affect you, but everyone else connected to you. On the contrary, when in alignment everything connected to you functions properly.

Ask Yourself:

1. What is out of alignment in your life?

2. Do you need to revisit your vision statement for realignment?

3. What steps will you take to get realigned? If you are in alignment, what will you do to stay on track?

DAY 15

PURPOSED OVER POPULAR

I n school, students tend to separate themselves into groups based on those who best mirror who they feel they are or who they want to be. In every school, there is what's considered the "popular" kids. These are the ones who seemed to be most liked by their peers for maybe academics, athletics, or even just social status. Do you remember them? We all had that popular crowd, and some of us were even part of that self-proclaimed "in-crowd".

What Really Matters

The irony of that entire era in school is that despite all the perks of popularity, such as recognition and attention, at the end of the day none of that even mattered. The real purpose of school was never contingent on anything related to popularity. Sometimes, we're still like children and carry this mentality over into adulthood as we seek after what will make us famous, and not what will make us purposeful. Sometimes we struggle with acceptance.

As described in Maslow's hierarchy of needs to reach "self-actualization," we often get stuck on our need to love and be loved by others. In return, we put forth all our efforts in hopes to accomplish something that will prove our worth and value to others and not to ourselves.

To the same effect, just because something seems to be popular or "trending" doesn't mean it's for you! Social media is a perfect example. Don't be fooled by the number of social media likes and shares. Everyone is posting success and what they think people want to see, but no one is posting about their flaws and failures. Never use something so shallow as a measuring tool for popularity. Many people are popular but have no real purpose for it.

Tying it all together

Again, this goes back to being in alignment with what you say you want and what you truly believe in. Your level of popularity will not serve your purpose because functioning in your purpose will catapult you into places reputation may take you, but can't sustain you. Popularity is temporary, but the discovering of your goal is permanent.

Don't spend your life trying to impress the very people who more than likely will not like you or even support you anyway. The purpose will not always be popular. Don't think you're losing because you're doing something different. There is a particular saying that goes, "Don't get the popular circle confused with the winner's circle." At best, pursue purpose and not popularity.

Ask yourself:

1. Do you value popularity over purpose? If so, how do you plan to fix this?

2. How much do you value the opinions of others?

3. Have you gained better insight into your purpose?

DAY 16

CONQUERING COMFORT

When I first began my journey as a fitness enthusiast turned amateur bodybuilder, I had to learn to adapt to the discomfort of the pain I went through. What I discovered was before my muscles could grow and develop, I had to endure the uncomfortable feeling of my muscle fibers being stretched to the point that it was no longer bearable. This was most felt during what's called drop sets or burnouts, when you keep lifting and performing the exercise until you reach a burnout or limit. For me, if at any point in time during my workouts I felt too comfortable with the weights, it meant my body had gotten adjusted to the program. One of the principles I live by that has aided in my success is to always position myself in a place of discomfort. I have become comfortable with being uncomfortable, and that keeps me productive.

You never know what you're capable of until you push yourself passed complacency. Once you push yourself, stay consistent in doing so. All too often, we get caught up in the same routine day in and day out. We are afraid to take a chance on something new, even if it has the potential to produce the results we truly want. Ask yourself, "When was the last time I did something different for the first time?" Get uncomfortable and take courage!

Create through discomfort

Although the idea of growth and change sounds good, I can tell you with confidence that it does not feel good. Just like when I'm trying to squeeze out that last heavy repetition of weights and the "ugly" begins to spread all over my face, your discomfort too is not always going to look good or feel better. Nevertheless, pump out those goals! It is those moments of pain and discomfort that will make you question if you're going down the right path! When this happens, remember why you started in the first place.

You must ask yourself if choosing comfort is worth forfeiting what you're creating. If it is, then by all means keep doing what you're doing. But if you are ready to give up the culture of your routine to grow, then adapt to the discomfort.

Nothing productive or impactful has ever come from a place of complacency and comfort. If I were satisfied with the outcome and results of my life, I would never have stretched myself to do more or discover my passion for impacting more. If I'd never stepped out of the boat, I would never have known I could walk on water. You should constantly find new ways to become uncomfortable. That moment of discomfort may be precisely what you need to tap into the potential and the gifts lying dormant on the inside of you. You are more creative than you think. You are just too comfortable.

Ask yourself:

1. When was the last time you made yourself uncomfortable?

2. What areas in your life do you know you should be maxing out, but you are doing the bare minimum?

3. What is that new thing you want to try but haven't? When do you intend to try it?

DAY 17

DISPOSING OF DISTRACTIONS

After enduring an intense 45-minutes of bumper-to-bumper standstill traffic, I slowly drove by what seemed to be the cause of the delay. From what I could see, what once was a fiery red exotic sports car was now reduced to the size of a miniature clown car that you see at the circus. It was communicated to onlookers that the driver of the once pristine car, now reduced to nothing, had taken his eyes off the road for a split second to attend to his phone.

Before he even realized it, he'd lost all control of the wheel and destroyed one of his most precious and prized possessions—something I'm sure he had invested a lot of time and money into obtaining and preserving.

We spend immeasurable time, energy, labor, and prayers into building things like our brand, business, family, reputation, relationships, or whatever it may be. Sometimes all it takes is one small vice to draw our attention away from our reality. I like to call it a catalyst for catastrophe. In any given moment, years of hard work can be erased by a distraction if precautions are not taken.

We can be so easily distracted by things that have absolutely nothing to do with our goals, when we lose sight of the bigger picture and allow ourselves to be drawn away from our desired outcome. And for what?! Is the distraction ever really worth it? In comparison to something you have invested your life and time into obtaining and maintaining, it's easier to cut it off — no need to lose it all on the whims of insignificance.

Distractions come our way in so many forms, that we almost can't decipher what's necessary from what's excessive. These distractions can include certain people, environments, thoughts, and even desires. Yes, even our desires can be a distraction because they occasionally coincide with our weaknesses and that which we know is good to us, but not good for us. I want to consider it as our guilty pleasures that we choose not to talk about. For some, this is food that is counterproductive to their health, yet we give in to the craving every time. Maybe it's the group of friends that do not see your true value neither do they see their own, yet they always manage to entice you with all the right words. Different vices can be subtle, so by the time you catch them the damage has already been done just like that driver who appeared to have everything under control until it was too late. Sometimes, all it takes is a quick lapse of judgment and a loss of focus. To counter this, we must always be sensitive and self-aware of possible changes.

Ways to eliminate?

- Create disciplines for your life. Desire without discipline only creates delays.

- Set up daily/weekly routines and regimens that you can stick to.

- Turn off technology when you're working on something specific to avoid multitasking.

- Limit your pleasures to specific times.

- Prioritize who and what's important.

- Allocate time to what needs to be done on your list of priorities.

If you think something is even potentially a distraction, examine it. Distractions come to destroy and deter you from your destiny. Always ask yourself if it's worth it.

Ask Yourself:

1. What are the major or minute distractions in your life?

2. Where could you be if you didn't let those things distract you?

3. What is the one distraction you are going to work on eliminating today?

DAY 18

SELFLESS TO SELFISH

From the distorted intercom looming above my head I could hear the words of the kind stewardess as she gave invaluable information. "Not that we expect this problem, but if for any reason there is a drop in the cabin air pressure the panels above will open, and oxygen masks will fall from the ceiling for all to carefully place it over their face. If you are with a child or someone else needing assistance, be sure to secure your mask first before helping anyone else." Well, that sounded pretty selfish, right? Or so I thought.

We are given numerous glory stories praising the undeniably heroic feats of others at the risk of their own lives. We're generally taught that having our moral compass pointed towards the north is being selfless and putting the needs of others before our own. Yet, in an aircraft, it is completely socially acceptable to put the needs of an individual above the needs of everyone collectively. The question then is, is putting myself first an act of heroism opposed to putting my neighbor's needs first?

How it applies to you:

Many of us devote our lives to the service and sacrifice of everyone but the right one, ourselves! From my personal experience, I know that the same burden we constantly carry for others is the very burden that can break our own back and cause us to burn out. There is such a thing as becoming so selfless to the extent you become the anchor of safety for others and somehow manage to drown yourself. In theory, you cannot save the world until you have saved yourself first.

Saving yourself and becoming selfless begins with first prioritizing your life and placing your needs above others' wants. Women usually tend to have this problem the most because they are nurturers, caregivers, mothers, friends, and companions. We tend to wear as many hats as it takes to keep someone else's head warm. Don't get me wrong, the same can be said of men as they tend to carry a God-like complex that often makes them feel as though they should always be the hero of everyone's story and the knight in shining armor. This is not a positive self-image because it only promotes selflessness without a balance of selfishness.

Practice Self-Care

The easiest way to overcome such complexes is to learn that saying no is sometimes necessary. People can drain every bit of life, liberty, and energy you have, leaving you dry and empty. You cannot be everything to everyone. Often, the very thing we try to breathe life into can leave us gasping for air. This is why you must secure the mask first!

Learn how to set boundaries for yourself and maintain your standards at all times. People will respect you as much as you respect yourself. If you do not set limits, they won't know when they are crossing them. It is ultimately your responsibility to save yourself! There is no way to effectively operate and function on what you need for yourself if everyone else's needs consume you.

Take time for yourself to make sure you are ok! Repeat after me, "It is ok, to not be ok." Sometimes, we get so busy in the hustle and grind mentality until we bypass the fact that we need to rest. This doesn't mean stop, it means making sure we are taking care of our holistic health, which includes:

Mind: If you need help or someone to talk out important issues with, it's a fantastic thing to seek therapy or counseling. This may appear as a taboo topic in our generation, but I assure you it's beyond helpful. In addition to preserving your mental state, you must feed your mental. What was the last book you read (besides this one)? Find stimulating podcasts, shows, documentaries, or even conferences to attend that can fuel and feed your growth and personal development. Tone down reality television and other things that are not cultivating your growth and character.

Body: Physically, make sure you are taking care of yourself, especially with what you put in your body. Maintain healthy habits and see a doctor not just when you have concerns, but before then. Create routines and regimens that you can stick to.

Spirit: Prayer and meditation will help calm your spirit and detox you from the negative energies you may encounter. Set aside a quiet time where there is nothing to distract you from finding a place of peace. This is a great way to refocus and center yourself.

We would all like to measure up to the heroic characters we hear about, but in reality we must be the heroine of our own life and save ourselves. Attempting to be the savior for everyone is not part of your purpose, neither is it your job. Burn out is real when it comes to your mind, your physical body, and even your spirit. Secure your mask, and then, if necessary, reach out to help others .

Also make sure you have something to pour from. How can you pour from a cup that is empty? The contents within the cup are specially made for you, and what you provide for others should be served from your overflow. When it comes to the initial question about being selfish or selfless, the answer is this, it is sometimes selfless to be selfish.

Ask Yourself

1.   What areas of your life are in need of more attention?

2.   When was the last time you practiced self-care?

3.   What can you do more of to ensure you are not burning yourself out?

DAY 19

MORE THAN MEDIOCRE

My early twenties are best defined as my years of discovery and self-development as I was unsure about what I wanted to do with my life. While I found myself discussing extravagant ideas about stepping out on purpose and creating a life of fulfillment, there was also a more dominant voice in my ear, drowning out the sound of my heart, and reminding me of the average life I was accustomed to living. This voice would always tell me, "You're doing too much. Be satisfied at the level you are on." The second voice reiterated that what I had purposed in my heart and mind to do was beyond conceivable for me to accomplish. This was the voice instructing me that it was perfectly acceptable to make the most out of my mediocrity. For a long time, I believed that and experienced little to no change.

Breaking out of a mediocre mentality will allow you to see yourself not just as you are, but as you should be. Sometimes those negative thoughts and voices arise to suppress the passion burning deep down on the inside of you. Mediocrity will tell you there is nothing special or phenomenal about you, and that you should be content with the way you are because that is where you'll always be. The problem isn't the voice, it is allowing what the voice is saying to settle in your spirit. I am here to affirm that you are more than mediocre. Shake the average dust that has sat there for quite too long, off your shoulders. Although you may not see the potential of what you possess that doesn't mean you don't possess something significant. Stop depriving yourself of walking out your best life because you don't feel you can function somewhere other than where you are. It was this same way of thinking that I had to overcome to write this book, and look at me now!

Affirmations

A good practice to enhance how you view yourself is to create personal affirmations. You may hear this word used a lot in todays culture. I can assure you that affirmations do work, if you work them! I personally practice affirming myself on a regular basis. This has aided so much in how I now positively view myself.

What are they? Affirmations are also known "I AM" statements. These are positive declarations you should consistently recite to yourself. Affirmations allow your mind to counteract the negative thoughts you may think about yourself. They help you in achieving success in all areas of your life because you are creating your world through the power of your words. It's not magic because you are simply doing the work to bring it to manifestation. As you create your affirmations, keep in mind that they should be:

- Personal, by using "I" or "My".

- Specific, not just generalized statements.

- Present tense. You want to begin manifestation now.

- Opposite. Think of a negative thought you have, and create the opposite thought to counteract it.

Don't let insecurities cause you to settle for a life of mediocrity, because honey there is nothing mediocre about you! You have to tap into your true self to experience a new level. This comes first by believing in yourself. Believe that when you walk out of those doors into the world, that you carry the weight of greatness and not mediocrity. Don't go by what you see, but by what you feel to be true. This entails building confidence. Truthfully, all you need is a little confidence to get the momentum going and get mediocrity GONE!

Ask yourself:

1. What or who in your life has made you feel like you were mediocre?

2. What are some positive affirmations you can use to boost your self-confidence?

If there is one thing I know about you, the fact that you are reading this book means there is something special about you, and you know it, or else you wouldn't have made a choice to invest in your personal growth. I challenge you to begin affirming yourself daily. Tell yourself, "I am phenomenal! I am amazing, and I was made to do great things." Don't live life little! Don't settle for less! If you choose to take that step, you have to believe in yourself, and if you don't like it, you can always go back to a mediocre mentality. But I promise once you've taken the road less traveled, you won't want to go back.

DAY 20

GRIND AND GROW

When a farmer sets out to produce a crop of any kind he has already set in his mind the time, energy, effort, and resources it will take to get what he desires. He has also orchestrated and counted the cost of what it will entail before he can see the crop produce. If you take off the last three letters in the word planted, you are left with the word "plan", meaning the farmer has a preconceived plan on the work it will take before he sees his crop bear fruit. He knows there will be good weather and there may even be foul weather. He considers the fact that he will have to till and cultivate the ground. He's even aware of the constant watering, monitoring, and ultimately waiting that must happen before any real growth takes place.

Just like the farmer, once you've gained the motivation, inspiration, and insight needed to conquer and claim your day and your life, I'd be remiss not to tell you this one detail, you must work for it before you sit back and wait for it.

Being inspired alone is not enough to sustain the process of getting the most out of your life. You must grind for it before you can get the desired growth from it. The faith to believe it must be coupled with the grind to receive it. Accomplishments don't just fall from heaven! Believe me. I waited a long time to see, but to my dismay, it never happened. I had to put some grind behind what I wanted to be mine.

Success comes from the grind and the sacrifice. Yes, there are some things we are blessed with, but to sustain any blessing, you'll have to do your part. Till the ground, cultivate the soil, and water the dream. Until you become the hard-working person you need to be, you will never receive the reward you want to see.

Working Over wanting

I used to live in this alternate reality in my mind which led me to believe that I only needed to hope and wish and believe that what I wanted would come to me just because! Let me tell you how miserable those years were for me. I had to become a farmer for my crops. To plant, I had to create a plan first. Then, I had to work the plan even if it meant working it by myself. So I did just that. No one around me knew what I was working towards or building, but I didn't expect them to because they weren't there when I planted the seed. But because I knew I had planted the seed in the ground, I had no choice but to work until it showed up. I was no longer expecting the growth to just happen. Success doesn't just happen. It is the creation of continued work and energy put into something until it is manifested. Grind is the work behind the wish. It is what separates the doers from the thinkers. Grinding is the process of simply working hard towards the desired outcome. You cannot put in a minimum amount of effort and expect a maximum amount of results. That won't work.

My personal formula for growth is simple:

Grace + Grind + Grit = Growth

Grace: Oftentimes we wonder why certain things we desire don't always work out as we would like. This is because you can only excel at something you have been graced to do.

Grind: This is where your part comes in. Once you know what you have been gifted the ability to do , then it is up to you to put the work behind it. This step can only be carried out by you!

Grit: This will determine how bad you want it. Grit is something internal that doesn't allow you to quit. This is allows you to work through even during the hardest of situations when you'd rather give up.

If you can equally incorporate all parts to your life, then execute becomes a lot easier and growth is inevitable.

Ask Yourself

1. What areas of life are you not putting forth the maximum effort?

2. What parts of the growth formula could you use more help in? How do you plan to execute on that?

DAY 21

STRENGTH FROM THE STRUGGLE

Wobble, wobble, wobble a little more.... fall...repeat. This was the pattern I watched as my niece made her first few attempts of at standing up. She struggled as her tiny knees and fluffy golden legs fought to keep their balance in hopes of sustaining her cute teddy bear body. I watched this same repetitive struggling motion day after day wishing that I could do it for her. This persisted for weeks until one day she managed to slowly pull herself up by placing one hand on the couch and the other tightly wrapped around my left index finger. As she maintained her stability, I slowly watched as the fingers were pulled back from her, and to her surprise she successfully stood tall on her own two legs.

Without the consistent struggle to stand my niece would never have gained the strength she needed in her legs to be able to stand. As much as I wished I could just come along and somehow make her legs strong enough to sustain her healthy frame all on their own, I just couldn't do that. I had to allow her to experience the struggles of learning to stand up on her own.

Lesson:

Sometimes it's the "help" that's hindering you. Growth and progress are never instantaneous nor easy, but eventually you'll reach the mastery of standing on your own. You'll never find your strength if you're always looking for a way out of the struggle.

The very area you struggle in may be leading you to what you have a burden for. For me, I struggled with finding my purpose and my voice. Because of those struggles, it gave me a passion for helping others get through the same thing. There were many other personal struggles I experienced before fully operating in my gift — struggles that I would never trade to be where I am right now. I look back, and I am so grateful for them.

Today's Struggle is Tomorrow's Strength

Believe me when I say that there is nothing like a good struggle story to highlight your success. Just consider the people you look up to the most and think of all the challenges they faced to become who they are. I guarantee they would tell you it was their struggles that helped lead them to their place of purpose. Many times, we are drawn to them as a result of what they experienced and how they overcame it. Accomplishing something is easy when there is no opposing force causing doubt and regret. Where's the lesson in that? Show me your struggle and I can better understand your strength.

What are you going to share with someone who is on a path that you have never conquered yourself? The purpose you are searching for is being developed during the *STRUGGLE*. The good news is, when you tough it out, you discover that you are stronger than your struggle. This is the foundation upon which character is created, and success is sought and built upon.

Remember, don't let life or career take you where your character can't keep you. Today's struggles can become tomorrow's strengths if you let it. Just know its ok to struggle because you're going to gain strength and experience in the process. What's not ok is quitting as a result of it.

Ask Yourself

1. What are you currently struggling with right now?

2. How can you use this struggle to your advantage?

3. What parts of your character can this situation help you build?

DAY 22

PUSH PAST IT

Push! Push harder! You're almost there! Breathe! Keep breathing! These are the words of the nurses and doctors coaching a mother as she delivers her baby. One of the most joyous moments for a mother comes the moment she holds the precious life she has fought and labored to bring into the world.

It's interesting that out of all the pain and agony that the mother may have experienced, not for a moment does she stop pushing! She knows the life of that child is contingent on pushing harder. If she doesn't tire and retire from processing the pain, she will have what she's waited nine months for. Holding her baby in her arm, she ultimately forgets all the pain she endured for the pleasure of what she now gets to experience.

There's Purpose in It

No one particularly likes or enjoys pressure. However, like everything else purposeful, it's producing in you what is needed to make you prosper. Don't abort your purpose because you are experiencing pain. Sometimes it's the pain in your life that is leading you to your divine purpose. My greatest place of pain was what catapulted me to start living and operating in a life that revolved around purpose. Before the pain, I didn't even know what I was supposed to do with my life outside of working a job to pay bills and provide for all my necessities. I was pushed into my purpose! That is a beautiful pain that I wouldn't trade for all the comfort in the world.

It may seem like what you are experiencing is not going to yield any return, but if you just give it time, you may be surprised at what comes out of it. You are experiencing labor pains because something has been growing on the inside of you and it is almost time for it to come forth. Don't abort the purpose! The pain has almost become like contractions getting closer and closer together. This is an indication that your delivery date is approaching and that it's time to birth what's been growing. When you feel the discomfort, don't diminish it because there is something in there.

Push Past What?

To that secret mind battle that tries to overtake your subconscious mind, push past it. To the financial struggle you seem to find yourself in every time you seem to be afloat, push past it. The brokenness of dreams and expectations that have not come to full term just yet, push past it. The thought that what you have planned to do may fail, push past it! If you give up now, you will never know the possibilities of what could be ahead! The consummation of pain is inconsequential to the reward of the promise.

Consider what you're up against. Are you enduring a temporary pain for a permanent promise? Or are you aborting a lasting purpose because of temporary pain? The pain you feel may be inevitable, but the suffering can be optional. Only those with that goal in mind will continue to push until they pursue greatness. Pain is nothing when your purpose is at stake. Convert that pain to power!

Ask Yourself:

1. What areas of your life are you experiencing the most pain?

2. How can you reverse your pain to become your power?

3. What can be aborted in your life if you don't get through the pain?

DAY 23

THE PATIENCE PROCESS

Have you ever experienced any injury such as a broken foot or a burn? Do you recall how after that injury occurred, you had to give it time before it went back to normal? You understood that it was going to take time to heal. You fully expected a healing process you would have to go through no matter how much of an inconvenience it was for you.

It is amazing how many processes in this lifetime we not only expect, but experience. We gladly accept them as being part of life. There is the birthing process, the healing process, the growth process, and the list goes on. Practically everything in life undergoes a process of some sort. We trust and firmly believe in them. The irony of us imagining the processes seem to always exclude the patience process.

You know the broken foot will take time, care, and attention to heal, but even then total recovery is not fully guaranteed. The process can be painful, disturbing, and exhausting. We're willing to wait patiently because we feel like we have no other choice. The problem is we don't have the same concept of patience while facing unexpected changes. Neither do we consider the necessary time required to reach an internal growth and external success. We expect instantaneous miracles or even magic to take place on a whim. Remember, the day you plant the seed is not the same day you reap a harvest.

The lack of patience for the process can even be attributed to what the world deems an "overnight success." This concept has drastically desensitized our ability to endure the developmental process that must take place. There will be days when you look at the lives of others and think that what has taken them practically a short amount of time to build or become is taking you a lifetime.

This is simply an illusion. You cannot see a plant growing every single day. However, when you give it time and check back, you will certainly notice the difference.

Nothing Overnight

No one discovered and tapped into their purpose overnight. Not even me! I have been on this journey of discovery for many years. It took a lot of prayer, pressure, pain, and patience even to get this far! I felt as though I would never find what was in God's design for my life. I looked at every setback or obstacle as destruction and delay. They were so much more than that.

Often your expectations are purposely delayed, but it does not mean they have been denied. What you rate as delay is helping you to become more developed and closer to your purpose. Be patient with not just your circumstances, but with yourself! If you know you are doing the best you can right now, stop putting yourself under unnecessary stress. Time is not in your control.

Time vs. Timing

Too much emphasis is placed on time and less emphasis on timing. In other words, everything you are after and searching for will happen in due time, not on your timing! You won't always be able to measure it by your watch or calendar. Just know it's going according to schedule. I can assure you time will not run out on you. Go back to where we discussed Fixing your Focus. Shift your perspective from how long it seems to be taking.

Tips for practicing patience

- Trust the process even when you can't trace the process.

- Remember to remain focused, steadfast, and consistent in all that you do.

- SLOW DOWN! Stop rushing everything! Just take your time and pace yourself.

- Retrain your brain to unlearn certain negative behavioral patterns. Don't accept them as being a part of who you are.

- Breathe! Just breathe. This will calm your spirit and help to focus you just as you feel yourself becoming overwhelmed or flustered.

Ask Yourself:

1. What is that area of my life that I tend to rush or get impatient in?

2. What will I choose to start doing today to help develop patience?

DAY 24

DEAR DREAMER

Can you remember being a child and knowing what you wanted to be? The possibilities were infinite. Nothing and no one could convince us that what we dreamt in our hearts was not, in fact, real or attainable. Our passions and frivolous desires were as real as the sky we looked up to and the ground we walked on. Whether it was an astronaut, a doctor, or even a superhero, we were 100% confident it was exactly what we would be! We possessed no knowledge of fear nor any concept of the word "unrealistic". We were completely oblivious to what "reality" meant, and were perfectly content with it. So how did we deviate so far from all of that because now we give up on dreams without a second thought.

And if the dream killers don't get to us first, our lack of drive and enthusiasm will. We have been dreaming for as long as we can remember, but it's not enough to dream, you must also work! Anyone can be a dreamer, but not everyone is an executor! The great thinkers and dreamers of time did more than sleep, dream, and repeat the process. They put action behind the dream. You have to be willing to work for the manifestation. Become great or stay average—the choice is yours. It is tough, but it is also very worth it and attainable.

Many times I could hardly sleep at night because my mind was swarmed with thoughts, words, and ideas, and I had no clue how to put them into the right use! I didn't even know the purpose of hearing them in my head. It became so overwhelming until what was meant to be a peaceful dream turned into a tormenting nightmare. I wasn't in tune with my purpose, and so I became a prisoner to what should have been my promises. Even those around me were blind to the dream in my head trying to manifest before my eyes. I had to remind myself that I can only see my dreams when I close my eyes, so it was unfair to expect someone else to see it on my behalf. I could not allow those dreams to simply slip through my grasp because of self-doubt and unbelief.

This is what happens if you sit on a dream. Dreams are an indication of your passion, which is waiting to be fulfilled as a purpose.

What Happened?

Somewhere along the line, something or someone convinced you that dreaming was only for sleepers, yet we have all not only heard, but are living the infamous, "I Have A Dream Speech". This is because everything you will ever accomplish starts with a dream. The only difference is that it doesn't stay there. The dream is just the early phase of what could be a full blown reality. What would you do if you knew you could not fail? What dream would you live out if you stopped listening to the voices of those who gave up on their dreams?

Dear dreamer, hold on to your dream! Don't sell out for society or the satisfaction of someone else who didn't make it through. Don't buy into the false hopes and superficialities that this life wants to offer. You are the prototype to your dream and vision, so never become the duplicate of someone else's! Don't even program your mind to think you can't wake up from that dream and make it a reality.

Learn to trust yourself and your capabilities. The place in your mind that is housing fear, doubt, and insecurity is the same place dreams die! Clear that negative space. Cultivate an environment of positivity that will speak LIFE to your hopes and dreams. Your dreams are sometimes the only reminder that what you want is real. You must go through the process of manifesting what you can't yet see. Above all else, don't stop dreaming.

Ask Yourself:

1. What dreams have I been dismissive of?

2. Why am I so afraid of making it my reality?

DAY 25

HIGHER HEIGHTS

I took my first solo flight about a year ago to visit family in the deserts of Arizona. From the window seat of the plane, it seemed as if it would take us forever to ascend from the rough, bumpy runway into the smoothed vast sky above. Once we did, it was amazing how all the objects that were once enormous seemed to dissipate until they finally disappeared. It was an uncanny correlation to life.

Like that plane rolling along the runway preparing for takeoff, sometimes it seems as if we are off to a pretty slow start, rolling along with life's track. We seem to be living in slow motion while everything else is simply passing us by. We feel nothing is happening for us and the destination is nowhere in sight. We never consider that the slow start is what we need to gain the necessary momentum and speed before ascending into the higher heights we envision.

You were designed to take flight and excel in every area of your life. I know sometimes that's hard to perceive when you are still operating from the ground or from a bottom place. But there will come a point in life will come when you will retract the wheels that have kept you down and do what you were created to do. Right now circumstances and life have got you thinking as low as the ground you're still on.

Elevation

You must learn to first elevate your mind before you can elevate your life. This elevation of course will go along with a separation of thoughts, feelings, and even people who are not living up to the level of your mission. When you see things from the point of view of a pilot and not a pedestrian, those issues that once seemed so insurmountable will soon become minuscule. Once you have ascended, stay high and aim for more. When you begin to come down, those same issues and mentalities you left behind will still be waiting for you.

Understand that you are just passing through these obstacles to get to your purposed destination. Not only do you have to look above, but you must also see beyond what is seen right now, and realize that just because you can't see it, doesn't mean you can't attain it. Just because you're experiencing turbulence doesn't mean you should turn back. You are simply paying the price for purpose.

Pilot Perception

When you are viewing your life and your future, try taking on the perception of the pilot. Although you can't see exactly what's going on, trust your internal GPS to get you there. Keep ascending higher. Even though it looks ugly now, everything will be much more beautiful at the top.

Ask yourself:

1. What areas of my life do I need to level up my thinking in?

2. What can I do to change the way I view my life and my purpose?

DAY 26

TURNING POINTS

You know the anticipation you get when you catch a glimpse of a seemingly amazing film? A film compiled with everything that's sure to make up a blockbuster hit. You finally watched the movie only to be taken on an emotional roller coaster from start to finish — an endless array of suspense, drama, comedy, tragedy, and triumph. So much so, until you feel as if you have become one with the protagonist of the story. What makes movies of this sort so successful are what writers consider to be the five key turning points. These five key points are what helps the character reach their resolution. These are the same key turning points that resonate with us. It's the "genetic make-up" of not only every great movie, but of our lives as well.

What are the points?

These turning points are known as Opportunity, Change of Plans, Point of No Return, Major Setbacks and finally the Climax. These elements make up the building blocks upon which the hero, us, must experience before reaching their goal.

We have to begin with the turning point of Opportunity. This is where we catch the first glimpse of what we feel will be a bright future. It's an exciting time when we've developed an idea or concept. It's when the opportunity forms into a clear-cut goal and objective, a change of plans eventually takes place. This is when you may have to rework the plan a bit, buts it's ok. After this, there is no turning back.

You are now at the point of no return, where you couldn't give up even if you tried. It's like entering the birthing process, and there's no stopping that baby now. My point of no return was when I began creating this guide. Although I faced discouragement along the way, I had already started and had made a commitment to finishing the project. I couldn't stop even though I faced multiple setbacks.

Don't Let the Setback Make you Turn Back

Sometimes just one setback may seem to create a domino effect. One thing after another may fall out of place. You may be experiencing that set back with your schooling, your relationships, or even with your job. In these moments, don't let your setback cause you to look back. The major setback was setting you up for the perfect comeback. This is when you know you're reaching a breaking point, which is the climax.

The climax of your favorite movie is the final and pivotal point when the heroine is faced with the greatest obstacle. This is when the question is posed, "What will he/she do now?" You are the heroine of this story, so no one else can answer this question but you! If you don't like the direction of your life's story, then rewrite it! It doesn't have to end that way. Have the same fight and determination for the fictional characters of your favorite movie as you have for yourself!

Ask Yourself:

1. What has been the major turning point in my life?

2. What setbacks have I encountered and overcome?

DAY 27

CORRECT CONNECTIONS

A not so secretive fact about me is that I am attached at the hip to my technology. I have a special and constant relationship with my devices, which forces me to constantly check them throughout my day. You can imagine what this does to my battery life even while on low-power mode. So I always have to make sure I keep my phone charged. One time I left my original cell phone charger at home, so I decided to swing by the store to pick one up. The new charger was a type I had never used before, and it appeared to fit my connector and that was all that mattered. After leaving the device connected for a couple of hours, I finally disconnected my phone from the charger. To my complete and utter dismay, instead of having a fully charged battery ready for immediate usage, I ended up having less charge with nearly no battery life. I was completely baffled as to how this was even possible with a brand new connector.

"It's impossible to be correctly connected to something and not experience the full charge and energy it is supposed to give."

The Explanation

Although my phone was connected to a charger, it was not connected to the correct charger. I later learned I had used what is called a universal charger, instead of the specific charger made for my phone. Although it appeared as if it was charging, in reality it was draining the life out of my phone. Sound familiar?

Have you ever wondered why you dread being in the presence of certain people and you leave mentally and emotionally drained? This is an incompatible connection at work.

When I knew that there was more for me to do and become, I began seeking out people who could help me tap into it. I didn't have the whole picture just yet, but I knew that if I wanted to be someone I've never been before, I would have to associate with people who I had never associated with before. It doesn't mean I completely forsook everyone, but it did mean that I had to let go of a few people, places, and ideas that were limiting my progress and not igniting my engine. You'll be able to identify them because you dread to come around and you leave drained. This is because there is no mutualism in the situation.

Connect

People who have found their purpose and know who they are have a different outlook on life, compared to those who haven't. They talk differently, live differently, and function differently. Everything about them is unique. It is the same for those who have set specific goals for the life they are trying to achieve. Being around purposed people provides certain energy that you need for your own life. These are the types of people you need to surround yourself with. They may not even be in the same field, niche, or industry you are interested in, but they can still provide you with helpful advice and insight. Usually, if a correct connection does not know the answer to something, they can help you find someone who does.

Find yourself a mentor, coach, or even someone who inspires you. Ask them to take you under their wings or guide you. I still invest in my purpose and growth by surrounding myself with a community of likeminded individuals, as well as a coach who has been where I am trying to go. These people will also pour energy that will never leave you drained.

Ask Yourself:

1.   What is that thing I am connected to that is not producing or aiding my growth?

2.   What do you dread that leaves you drained? How can you limit this from happening?

3.   Who do you need to position yourself with to help you reach your goals?

world around you. Nelson Mandela did not reluctantly fight to end discrimination. He was intentional in loving his oppressors and offering forgiveness.

- Become less consumed about viewing your actions as being a "good look". Do something within your lifetime to have an impact for a lifetime! Strive to live the legacy you want to leave. This requires living out your dreams and living them out from your core. Living from the inside-out will far outlast living a life from the outside. Live from the side people do not only see but that they can feel too!

- Remember, your purpose and your life are not just about you, so stop living selfishly! If your intent for discovering your destiny is for the sake of staking a claim to fame, to pacify insecurity, or to prove others wrong, then you should reevaluate your life. The identity and destiny I'm helping you to discover is one that will impact this generation and generations to come.

- Plant seeds with your life that will leave a harvest for any and everything that is connected to your soil.

You don't have to be named among the greats like Nelson Mandela to do something great! Your legacy will always be connected to your value. Your convictions and what you believe should continuously be represented. Nelson Mandela epitomized peace and justice because he lived his life fighting for it. This is what he represented while he was alive. What do you epitomize and represent when others see or think of you? How do you treat other people and what impression are you leaving?

"I've learned that people will forget what you said, people will forget what you did, but people will never forget how you made them feel."- Maya Angelou

Ask Yourself:

1. How will you use your core values to create your legacy?

2. What do you want your legacy to be?

3. What living legacy have you already begun to create?

4. What are you known for?

DAY 29

PRIVATE PARTY

You've been focused. You've been consistent. You have been dedicated to your growth and development. You've got to know that you've come a long way from where you first started. When was the last time you threw a party? That's right! When was the last time you celebrated the one person you spend all day and every day with? The one person you've been building, learning, and discovering more about life with. When was the last time you celebrated YOU?

As you're journeying, grinding, discovering yourself and your destiny, it's easy to neglect yourself in the process. I know we mentioned practicing self-care earlier, but now it's time to take it to a new level. When you are a selfless, hard-working person, you may also have a natural propensity to celebrate the achievements of others, but only tolerate the manifestation of your own. As soon as we hear about a party or celebration of a friend or loved one, we make plans, arrangements, and even pick out outfits to show our support of them. The only party we choose to attend for ourselves is one of self-pity.

We reflect on everything that hasn't happened for us or that hasn't worked out. We pilfer through the Rolodex of our minds replaying failed attempts and reliving disappointing scenarios. We let life rain on our parade.

Understand that your life will already come equipped with roadblocks, mistakes, and obstacles, but these are all stepping stones to our desired destination. None of us are without faults or failure, but we are learning and not losing! It's time you celebrated milestones, moments, and positive memories. What a better way to celebrate than with a party?

How?

I'm not talking about literal balloons, confetti, cocktails, and candles, but if that's your preference, more power to you. What I mean is a time of solitude and silence. Set aside a time of lessons and reflections to commemorate the level you are on now and celebrate just how far you've come.

I know you've always been taught to allow others to acknowledge you. I agree with not boasting in yourself to the extent hubris begins to creep in. What I am saying is that it's ok to be proud of yourself without having pride attached to it.

By now you've self-assessed and engaged in many days of reflection. You've discovered those areas of your life that need improvement; and you've worked diligently to become a better you and to position yourself for your destiny. You've learned more about yourself than you may have known before. You have faced some big truths! This takes courage, tenacity, grit, and grind! I'm permitting you to praise yourself on purpose! Praise your strength, your fight, your faith, your trials, and even your triumphs. Life isn't the equivalent of grade school. You won't always have someone around that will pat you on the back and remind you that you're doing a good job. If you're waiting for that to happen, let me be the first to rain on that parade. You must learn to be your worst critic as well as your best encourager. Acknowledge that some days just being able to roll over and face the day shows a massive amount of progress. Celebrate that small win because when you do, you make room for greater wins to follow.

Ask Yourself:

1. What progress have I made during my journey thus far?

2. What are your small wins mentally, emotionally, in your career, and your family?

3. How do you plan to track and celebrate your growth ?

DAY 30

DESTINATION DISCOVERY

By now I hope you have gone through the process of uncovering, unlocking, and discovering what's on the inside of you. Come to grips with the validity that each problem, circumstance, and road block you will encounter while on your journey is purposed, if only you learn how to use it to your advantage.

Your destiny may look different from mine or even from those around you and closest to you. Nevertheless, be confident that in the end, if you trust your process, have patience, and keep your mind and spirit lifted, you will be just fine. I am only sharing with you some principles that have allowed me to experience drastic growth and change while on my journey to discovery — a journey that led me to my destiny.

The order and the timing of which you work through each principle will be circumstantial to where you are in this moment. Don't put yourself under pressure. Above all, have patience. Sometimes it's ok to put it on that top shelf until you come across it in time. At some point, you will most definitely encounter many things, especially if your vision is fixed far beyond what you can currently see.

Remember how we discussed perspective earlier in this book? Make sure you are looking beyond how things appear right now. Peer deeper into your future. Instead of perceiving the uncertainty of your journey with all its turning points as something negative, envision the growth and the development as part of a process leading you to what will be your greatest success story. No matter what you may encounter or face, if you firmly make the declaration, "This will work", and become adamantly consistent and persistent in your journey, the destination will be closer than it appears. Look at yourself as being the ultimate juggernaut- powerful, overwhelming, and unstoppable. There is no single difficulty or obstacle you will face that you won't be able to overcome.

Stand strong in your convictions and in what you hold to be true to your purpose! Don't waver and don't dare look back to where you have been. It is up to us to discover our ultimate self. This is a journey tailor-made for you. You have everything you need to get there. Take these principles, coupled with your persistence and resilience to conquer and complete everything you have set out to achieve. Carry on and remember to never stop discovering! There is now and will always be more to you than meets the eye. You owe it to yourself to find out what that more is!

DAY 31

THE RECIPROCATION

Once I got tired of waking up unfulfilled and unsure about my purpose and presence on this earth, I made the decision to seek for more. Was it easy? Absolutely not! Did I feel like I was in way over my head some days? Absolutely. Nevertheless, it was my intentionality that kept me holding on and pushing to my purpose. I no longer wanted to wake up and just "wing it". I wanted to be conscious of the life I was living and the decisions I was making.

Once I reached a place of peace and purpose, I realized it wasn't enough for me to achieve living my best life. I realized I owed it not only to myself, but to every other person who struggles in the areas where I have found my strength. I learned to execute on these principles. I needed to help someone else do the same.

The very last step I will give to you is one that has nothing to do with you, but everything to do with the person sitting next to you in class, at work, on the bus, or even standing in your circle of influence. When you succeed, everything connected to you will succeed as well. When you win, you should help someone else win. A true leader creates more leaders. I challenge you to reciprocate what has been given to you, information to live a more fulfilled life. Remember, life consists of lineage and legacy. A reoccurring theme of this guide has been that finding your purpose is not just about you, but about those you will impact.

The Challenge

At this very moment, someone you know is teetering on the precipice of purpose and gambling with their greatness. You may be the very catalyst they need to ignite that change. You may even need to refer back to a few chapters yourself before passing it along. That is completely ok to do.

Once you have completed this guide, I challenge you to share your process and the insight you've learned to develop someone you care about. Look for opportunities to pour into the lives of others. Give to someone else what you have just received. Reflect on each day and the lesson that came along with it. Don't just get the knowledge, make the knowledge applicable to your life. People should see the difference in you after executing what you have just discovered.

Ask Yourself:

1. What were your top 3 takeaways from this guide?

2. What knowledge have you gained that you didn't have before?

3. What did you learn about yourself?

4. When do you plan to execute on this information?

5. What parts of this guide do you need to revisit again?

6. Who do you know can most benefit from this book?

SPECIAL ACKNOWLEDGEMENTS TO A FEW VERY SPECIAL PEOPLE

1. David/Mary Kingcannon

2. Ashley Williford

3. Alexis Perry

4. Tiffany Bivins

5. Samantha Hill

6. Sharon Conner

7. Vickia Cullars

8. Jeanette Wright

9. Ashley Jones

10. Lauren Hawes

11. Anita Curry

12. Clevonna Jordan

13. Rebecca Majzer

14. Rosalyn Daniel

15. Benjamin Martin

16. Sara Bailey

17. 17.Kentrice Gaines

18. Brittany Jenkins

19. Mia Reid

20. Rafer Belton

21. Akiesha Taylor

22. Arthur Mealer

23. Ann Mosley

24. Cleopatra Andrews

25. Esi Krampah Kingcannon

26. Alice/Jesus Sostre

27. Samantha Hill

28. Seretha Sherrod

29. Anthony Jackson

30. LaCrystal Lockett

31. Daquicha Nathan

32. Marquita Williams

33. Felicia Asomaning

34. Charles Henderson

35. Kimberly Kingcannon

36. Doris Bacote

37. Rachelle McCain

38. Daphne Ali

39. Karol Moss

40. Lashiver Tanksley (LoLo Monroe)

41. BriAuna Ashley

42. Danielle Parks

43. Ashley Cullars

44. Jasmine Ryans

45. Cynthia Flores

46. Anthony Jackson

47. Julia Smith

48. LaWanda Foster

49. Chris and Chameka Bennet

50. Lawanda Foster

Made in the USA
Columbia, SC
29 June 2019